The Hope Chest:
The Amish of Ephrata

An Amish Novella on Morality

By
Sarah Price

Published by Price Publishing, LLC.
Morristown, New Jersey
2013

The Pennsylvania Dutch used in this manuscript is taken from the Pennsylvania Dutch Revised Dictionary (1991) by C. Richard Beam, Brookshire Publications, Inc. in Lancaster, PA.

Contact the author on Facebook at
http://www.facebook.com/fansofsarahprice or
visit her website at http://www.sarahpriceauthor.com

Price Publishing, LLC.
Morristown, NJ
http://www.pricepublishing.org

Other Books by Sarah Price

The Amish of Lancaster Series
#1: Fields of Corn
#2: Hills of Wheat
#3: Pastures of Faith
#4: Valley of Hope

The Amish of Ephrata Series
#1: The Tomato Patch
#2: The Quilting Bee
#3: The Hope Chest
#4: The Clothes Line (2013)

The Plain Fame Trilogy
Plain Fame
Plain Change (2013)
Plain Again (2013)

Amish Circle Letters
Miriam's Letter: Volume 1
Rachel's Letter: Volume 2
Leah's Letter: Volume 3
Anna's Letter: Volume 4
Lizzie's Letter: Volume 5
Sylvia's Letter: Volume 6
Lovina's Letter: Volume 7
Ella's Letter: Volume 8
Mary Ruth's Letter: Volume 9
Miriam's Package: Volume 10

The Adventures of a Family Dog Series
#1: A Small Dog Named Peek-a-boo
#2: Peek-a-boo Runs Away
#3: Peek-a-boo's New Friends
#4: Peek-a-boo and Daisy Doodle (2013)

Other Books
Gypsy in Black
Postcards from Abby (with Ella Stewart)
Meet Me in Heaven (with Ella Stewart)
Mark Miller's One Volume 11: The Power of Faith
A Gift of Faith: An Amish Christmas Story
An Amish Christmas Carol: Amish Christian Classic Series

A Christmas Gift for Rebecca: An Amish Christian Romance
Fields of Zombies: An Amish Parable (with Sam Lang)

Find Sarah Price on Facebook
http://www.facebook.com/fansofsarahprice
and Twitter @SarahPriceAmish

Learn about upcoming books, sequels, series, and contests!

*Dedicated to Lennon Baldwin
and his family.
No family should ever have to
go through what you have.
My heart and prayers are with you.*

Table of Contents

Chapter One

Priscilla sat in the attic, the battery-operated lantern on the floor casting a soft glow about the room. There was a large window that faced the east, which brought in bright sunlight in the mornings but deep shadows in the late afternoons. It was late March and the sun was setting on the western side of the farmhouse.

As the days had begun to warm up in March, she often snuck upstairs to the attic. The door always squeaked as she opened it, causing Priscilla to glance over her shoulder and make certain her mamm didn't spot her. Only after she knew that she hadn't been spotted, she would quietly steal up the creaky wooden stairs. Holding a battery-operated lantern in her hand, she would set it on the floor before the chest and, with shaking hands, she would reach down to open the lid.

Her daed had said that he would bring it downstairs in the springtime after the crops were planted. Then she could stare at the beautiful items that were held within the hope chest without worrying about her mamm seeing or her bruders teasing her. She didn't want to appear vain or proud. But her curiosity seemed to get the best of her, no matter how hard she tried to control it.

It was a beautiful hope chest, made of cedar wood and adorned with a carved heart on its front panel. Two birds flew toward either side of the heart, ribbons in their beaks. The hope chest was the symbol of every young Amish woman's dreams: two lives coming together for the very happiest future possible while living under the love and protection of the Lord. The carvings were not an expression of pride or vanity from the part of the maker or the recipient but rather a testimony to the sanctity of a girl's future wedding; an union that would perpetrate the traditional values engrained within the Amish community since centuries past.

Priscilla shut her eyes for a brief moment and breathed deeply. This summer, it would be two years since she had started courting Stephen Esh. That time seemed to have flown by quickly. During the first year, she had seen him without fail every other weekend. He made a point of stopping by the house to take her to the singings in the evenings following church service. Just this past autumn, Stephen had also begun to come visit on Saturday evenings when they didn't have church the next day. It had taken her a while to get used to him showing up at the house. Yet, her family accepted him into their hearts and home as if it was the most natural thing in the world.

For Priscilla, it was more than natural.

While he hadn't asked her yet, she knew that Stephen Esh was the man for her. He was the man she wanted to spend the rest of her life with, to have kinner and work the farm, to grow old and share in life's little joys. Stephen Esh was a good God loving man and she knew that their future would be long and bright.

Peering into the chest, Priscilla smiled as she saw the pretty embroidered tablecloth and handkerchiefs that she had added just the other week. Simple and white, the tablecloth would look pretty on her table for special occasions such as First Christmas and Easter supper. She had embroidered tiny flowers on the corners. It hadn't taken very long, especially since it had snowed so much that week. With the skies so grey and the air so cold, Priscilla was thankful for an excuse to remain inside where it was warm and work on her embroidering next to the family's old cast iron wood stove.

As to the handkerchiefs, she would take those in her pocket when she went to Sunday worship or singings. She had also made a few extra ones to give as gifts to her friends, Polly and Sarah. For those gifts, she had embroidered small sparrows, her favorite birds, along the edges. She would give those gifts to her friends when it was her wedding day, a special thank you for all of their support during the past year. It was a token of their friendship that had continued to grow, despite the best efforts of Susie Byler to make Priscilla look bad in the eyes of the community.

No, Priscilla thought. Even Susie Byler with her horrible falsehoods and accusations hadn't been able to drive a wedge between Stephen and her that first summer. Just as important, her friends had stood by her when some members of the community had wondered if there was any truth to Susie's mean and crazy attempts to discredit Priscilla as the good Amish woman that she strove to be.

For a moment, she shut her eyes and thought about the last time she had been with Stephen. Whenever he was near her, she felt light-headed with joy. The way he moved and the way he looked at her, even the way his eyes sparkled when he snuck a peek in her direction, made her pulse quicken. Oh, she thought, to be happily married to him at last and to begin their life together!

"Pricilla? You upstairs again?"

Startled out of her daydream, she quickly shut the lid of the hope chest. "Ja, Mamm." Resting her hand atop the chest, she stood up and hurried down the stairs. Her cheeks were flushed, embarrassed that her mamm had caught her, once again, in the attic gazing at the contents of the chest.

"Honestly, dochder," her mamm said when Priscilla walked into the kitchen. "A little less daydreaming would be right gut, ain't so?"

"Sorry, Mamm," Priscilla admitted as she set the table for the noon meal. She hadn't realized that it was so close to dinnertime and immediately regretted that she had left her mamm working alone for so long.

No sooner had Priscilla placed the last plate on the table than the door opened and her two brothers walked in ahead of their daed. Their cheeks were bright pink from the cold weather and their eyes bright from having been outside.

"Starting to warm up a bit, I think," Daed said as he washed his hands at the kitchen sink. "Fields are all plowed and ready for planting. Had a late start this year from all that snow."

Priscilla looked up, surprised by her daed's comment. "It's not too late, is it? Being almost April and all."

He shrugged. "Ja, a bit. The boys and I will get started early morning, seeing that the forecast is good for a few days."

Mamm looked at the calendar that hung on the kitchen wall by the refrigerator. "You plant now, you are only a week or so late, I reckon," she pointed out. "Not certain how that will make up on the backend for harvesting." She placed the bowls of piping hot boiled potatoes on the table and motioned for Priscilla to bring over the other bowls of hot food. "But it sure is nice to have warm weather once again."

Once everyone was seated, they bowed their heads in silent prayer. Priscilla thanked the good Lord for the food that

12

was on the table and the many blessings that He bestowed upon her family and the community. She barely heard her daed clear his throat, signaling the end of the pre-meal prayer.

For the next few minutes, plates were passed around, first to daed then to the boys before finally making their way to Priscilla and her mamm. The clinking of the mismatched tableware and bowls broke the silence as everyone filled their plates. The dinner meal was the heaviest meal on the farm. It would provide them all with energy to face the long afternoon of work, both in the house and in the barn.

"Bishop stopped by earlier," her daed said, breaking the silence as he began to cut a piece of the meatloaf.

Priscilla looked up and frowned at her daed. The bishop didn't often visit with the members of the community unless he was invited or unless there was a problem. Since no one had mentioned inviting the bishop to fellowship in the past few months, she had the sinking feeling that something was amiss.

"Ja?" Mamm responded, raising an eyebrow as she glanced from her husband to her daughter. Clearly, she was as surprised as Priscilla by the announcement. "A social visit during planting time?"

He hesitated before responding, taking the moment to savor the food. With his eyes shut, he smacked his lips together. "Your meat loaf," he started. "The best in the church district, if I may say so myself."

"Daed?" Priscilla prodded. "The bishop?"

He set his fork down and looked at her. "Ja, I did mention he stopped by for a visit," he started slowly. From the expression on his face, Priscilla could tell that it wasn't bad news and, for that, she was thankful. "Seems like the teacher got into a little accident and broke her leg."

Mamm gasped. "I hadn't heard any of that! When did this happen?"

"Just yesterday, it seems. School needs a replacement teacher until they let out at the end of May. Bishop Zook asked if you, Priscilla, might be able to step in to help."

For a long moment, the room fell silent. Four pairs of eyes stared at Priscilla and mouths hung open in wonder. To be asked to help the children, to be a teacher for the next two months, was not something to be taken lightly. It was a big job and quite an honor, especially after all of the Susie Byler fuss earlier in the winter and last summer.

"Oh my," Priscilla whispered. Her heart began to flutter inside of her chest. To be a teacher? To teach the children? She'd have to work outside of the home and away from the farm every day. She'd even work on some Saturdays, helping the older children with their journals and math, since they stopped attending school at eighth grade. "I've never taught before! Why would he ask me?"

Her daed shrugged as he lifted a fork loaded with meatloaf toward his mouth. "Don't rightly know why but he sure was confident that you'd be a right gut substitute."

"What did you tell him, Daed?"

Her father frowned and lowered the fork, shaking his head at his daughter. "Now, you know I'd no sooner commit you to something like that than I would make any other important decision for the family without discussion. It impacts more than just you, Priscilla," he pointed out. "Impacts all of us, truth be told."

"I don't know what to say," she replied softly and looked

at her mamm as if pleading for guidance. "I'd have Katie and Ben as students, too. Would they respect me as their teacher?"

Her mamm smiled. "That's up to you to insure that it happens, ja?" She reached over and touched Priscilla's hand. "But they are raised well. There's no reason that they wouldn't pay you proper respect."

"But who will help you with chores?" Priscilla asked.

"I can manage on my own. Plus, you'd be here in the afternoons to help," her mamm reassured her.

"Priscilla's going to be a teacher," Jonas teased. His older brother, David, nudged him to be quiet.

"You'd earn some money," Daed added. "Might be nice to have some extra cash on hand in case there is anything you need to buy in the upcoming year or so."

She knew exactly what her daed meant, despite not actually saying it. In early May, Priscilla would turn eighteen. Most likely, she'd take her kneeling vow in the autumn so that, if Stephen asked, she could marry him shortly after. Most young couples got married in November and December, although some couples were getting married in May to help break up the wedding season. With Stephen being older, she doubted he would want to wait much longer. So, to her daed's point, there would be a lot of extra expenses in setting up a new home together should that event take place. The next few months would go by quickly after all.

"I reckon I could do this," she said out loud but mostly to herself. "It can't be too hard."

"And you'd be helping those students who don't have a teacher right now," Mamm added. "It would be a good experience, too. One can learn a lot from helping others to learn." Clearly, her mamm approved of the idea and was trying to point out the positive aspects of the proposition.

Without further hesitation, Priscilla nodded her head and smiled. "Then I guess I'll be a teacher for the next two months!"

Daed looked as pleased with her decision as Mamm did. "After dinner, we'll ride to the Zook farm and tell them the gut news. You'll probably spend the rest of today reviewing teacher notes and lesson plans, I reckon."

Priscilla looked at her mamm, feeling guilty that the burden of the chores would fall on her alone. "I can help later this afternoon, Mamm."

"Don't you worry about a thing," her mamm said. "If you take this job, those students are your number one concern. Education is important."

Priscilla bowed her head down, humbled by this great task that had been offered to her. She knew that her absence from the house would be a burden to her mamm. After all, there were still a lot of chores to do, even with only three grown children living in the house. One day, David or Jonas would take a wife and live in the house, raising their families there and, eventually, taking over the farm. Then, Mamm wouldn't have so many chores to do or, at least, she would have some help from the new daughters-in-law and, eventually, their kinner.

"I understand, Mamm," Priscilla finally said humbly. "I won't take this responsibility lightly."

Chapter Two

The small cream-colored building seemed a lot different to Priscilla than when she had attended there two years ago. This time, she was walking toward it, not as a student but as a teacher. She could remember the many years that she had studied under the tree in the playground instead of playing on the swings with her friends. She had always loved school and studying. Reading and writing were always her favorite subjects. She loved reading the different books that the school let the children borrow, all approved by the church and families, of course. She certainly hoped that she could instill the same sense of respect for the different subjects as her teachers had done for her.

"Teacher's here!" one of the children yelled. Several children were already at the school, playing in the schoolyard. Two little girls, one in a blue dress and the other in a green one, sat on the front step by the door of the one-room schoolhouse. Their hair was neatly rolled back and pinned in a bun that was held under their prayer kapps. They looked up when they saw Priscilla approach the building and smiled.

"*Gut mariye*, Teacher," the one little girl said. Priscilla recognized her as Gideon Fischer's *dochder*, Lizzie.

"Hello Lizzie," Priscilla greeted her. "And *gut mariye* to you both."

Using the small key that the bishop had given her the previous evening, Priscilla unlocked the door and entered the building. It felt smaller than she remembered. Slowly, she walked down the aisle toward the front of the room. If she remembered correctly, the girls sat on the left side and the boys on the right. She wondered if the current teacher had changed that.

The room was bright and filled with sunshine. It was a warm and welcoming school with children's drawings on the walls and a big green chalkboard that filled the back wall. A happy place, she thought as she walked past the bookcase and ran her fingers along the spines of the books: The Story of the Bible, Singing Mountains, Pepper in Her Pie. She remembered some of those books from when she was in school, the pleasant stories that usually taught good values and strong morals.

On the wide windowsill, there was a pile of magazines called the Young Companion. Priscilla remembered that her own teacher used to read from them to the smaller children on Fridays. There were always lovely stories in there, short essays on how to distinguish a truly godly person or poems about friendship. There were even short stories about Bible verses. Priscilla couldn't wait until she had some time to pour through the older issues and pick out stories to read to the children.

The bishop had given Priscilla the lesson plans from the regular teacher who was apparently very organized. The teacher structured her days very similar to the way that Priscilla remembered her own school days: English and math in the morning before a short recess. Then reading before lunch. Writing and spelling were saved for the afternoon.

There were twenty children in the school, from a total of six families: four from the Millers, three from the Fischers, three from the Bylers, eight from two Lapp families, and her own sister's two children. There were fewer children than when she went to school there. The majority of children were younger which Priscilla thought would make it easier.

She was curious about the Byler children. They were cousins with Susie Byler, the mean spirited Amish woman who had bullied Priscilla last summer and then again in the winter. While she was familiar with the children from church, Priscilla didn't know them very well. She hoped that they were nicer than their cousin, that was for sure and certain.

At a quarter to nine, she walked through the door and called the children inside to get settled into their places. She felt nervous as she stood before the class, her palms sweating as she felt twenty pairs of eyes on her. Twenty children were watching her and wondering what type of teacher she would be. Priscilla was thinking the same exact thing.

"*Gut mariye*," she said as she took a deep breath. "I will be your teacher for the rest of the term. I know all of you from church so I do not need introductions. Your teacher left me detailed plans for the next few weeks but I will be asking all of you to help me as we get started into a new routine."

She looked round and no one spoke. They continued to stare at her, their eyes large and wide. Even Katie and Ben seemed to be watching her with a mixture of curiosity and awe.

"So, I think we should get started with a silent prayer and then a singing of a hymn," Priscilla said.

The room fell silent and every head bowed as the children prayed their silent prayers. Priscilla said her own prayer, praying for the Lord to guide her as she taught these children. She wanted to know patience and compassion and understanding. Teaching these children was a large responsibility. Their parents entrusted her with far more than just their education. The children were like small vessel and it was her job to help fill them with good values and godly morals. Priscilla was truly humbled by the honor to do so. Now, she thought, *if only God will walk beside me so that I can fulfill this duty to the best of my ability.*

As soon as the morning prayer ended, Priscilla looked up and surveyed the classroom. All eyes were on her, the children waiting for her guidance. She cleared her throat. "I think it would be right gut to start the day with a singing of the last two verses of Morning Thoughts. Do you know this song?"

She already knew the answer to that question. It was a lovely children's poem set to a tune that had been sung in the schoolhouse for years. It held the essence of what the Amish called *Gelassenheit*, the foundation of their religion calling for the believers to think of God first, others second, and themselves last.

So, when the children nodded their heads, she smiled brightly. "That's wunderbaar gut! Shall we begin, then?"

I must be a Christian child,
Gentle, patient, meek and mild.
Must be honest, simple and true,
In my words and actions, too.
I must cheerfully obey,
Giving up my will and way;
Must not always be thinking
Of what is pleasantest to me;
But must try kind things to do,
And make others happy, too.

If a playmate treats me ill,
I must be forgiving still;

I must learn my lessons well,
Not my schoolmates to excel,
But because my heart's delight
Is in doing what is right.
And in all I do and say,
In my lessons and my play,
Must remember God can view
All I think and all I do;
Glad that He can know I try,
Glad that children such as I,
In our feeble ways, and small,
Can serve Him who loves us all. [1]

When the children had finished singing the song, Priscilla smiled at them. "That was right lovely," she said. "And those are words that we can all reflect upon. Doing what is right makes us happy, deep inside our hearts, because God knows every thing that we think as well as all that we do."

Silence.

"Now, let us approach our lessons today with that same attitude of patience and cheerful obedience," she continued. "I'd like to start with the younger kinner among you, class. Since we are to practice our English in the morning, I thought we'd begin with reading this story from the Young Companion. While we are doing just that, the older students can begin writing an essay on what it means to be a Christian child."

The younger children came to the front of the room as Priscilla walked over to the bookshelves to select a copy of the Young Companion. She saw the cover and smiled. It was from

---

[1] The Friend of Youth and Child's Magazine, June 1859.

last winter, a lovely story called Bridled Thoughts, about a young girl who tried not to speak poorly of others but worried that her thoughts were not as pure as her actions.

"This is a gut story to practice our English," she said. "Let's start with Katie." Priscilla smiled at her niece. Handing her the magazine, Priscilla urged her to begin. "Could you read the first paragraph?"

Katie took the magazine and glanced down at the article. " 'The last notes of the parting hymn faded away. A stir filled the room as friends turned to chat with each other before heading home[2].' "

"That was good, Katie. Now tell me, what is the verb of that first sentence?"

"Faded?"

"Very good!" Priscilla beamed. "Now, let's have Morgan Byler take the next turn."

Katie hesitated, glancing first at Morgan, a small blond haired boy standing next to her, then back at Priscilla. "Morgan?"

"That's what I said," Priscilla responded.

With a big sigh, Katie handed him the magazine. Reluctantly, he took it from her and glanced down at the story. "You want me to read this?" he asked.

"Go on now."

He swallowed and held the paper before his face. He seemed to be studying the words but no sound came out of his mouth. "I...I can't make out the words," he said meekly, almost apologetic.

---

[2] From the February 2013 Young Companion.

Katie raised her hand.

Priscilla ignored her. "What do you mean that you can't make out the words?"

"They...they just look all jumbled to me. They don't make no sense," he said, averting his eyes. He looked ashamed and Priscilla felt her heart break inside of her chest. Something was wrong and she wasn't certain she could help the boy. But she knew that she would certainly try.

"Teacher!" Katie called out. She didn't wait for Priscilla to give her permission to speak. "Our other teacher always has Morgan copy passages to help him learn his words."

Priscilla took the magazine from Morgan and placed a gentle hand on his shoulder. "Never you mind, Morgan. You and I will work together later this morning. We can see if that helps, ja?"

He looked relieved that he didn't have to read anymore in front of the classroom. "Danke, Teacher," he said, his voice full of gratitude. Clearly, he didn't like being the center of attention in front of the other students.

Later that day, when the other children were outside during recess, Priscilla spent some time with Morgan, trying to help him with his reading. She even asked him to copy down the sentences that he was trying to read. When she looked at the paper, she was shocked to see that, indeed, the words were jumbled up. Instead of the word 'the', he had written 'teh'. Instead of the word 'hymn', he had written 'hmyn'. She had never seen anything like this before, that was for sure and certain.

"Well, we'll keep working on this," she said gently. "And, Morgan?"

He looked up, tears in his eyes. "Ja?"

"You have lovely penmanship. The finest I've seen in a long time," she said with a warm and caring smile.

The little boy looked up at her, his eyes wide and a grin rapidly spreading across his face. "Really?"

"Really!" she laughed.

"Oh, danke, Teacher!" he gushed.

He ran out of the school to join his friends in the yard. She walked over to the window and peeked outside, watching the children as they ran back and forth, chasing each other. Two of the little girls were playing on the seesaw, laughing in delight. The sounds of their voices and laughter warmed Priscilla's heart. She had never known such joy as she had that morning.

Indeed, she was looking forward to teaching these wonderful children over the next several weeks.

Chapter Three

To Priscilla's relief, she found that the students were quite cooperative and calm. She didn't have any problems with them during the school day. Even more impressive, Priscilla found that she enjoyed teaching. When she could help the children solve a problem or improve their writing and spelling, she felt a great sense of accomplishment.

She began to fall into a routine that balanced schoolwork and her chores at home. It wasn't too much extra work at all, she thought after that first week. Plus, her joy at working with the children and listening to their clever questions and funny stories were always adding an enjoying touch to the family conversations during the evening meal.

Before she knew it, three weeks had passed. When she had shut the school doors on Friday afternoon, she had looked around at the pretty flowers that the children had planted that week by the walkway. It had been an experiment that she had come up with on her own to explain the importance of education. Like flowers, education needed to be nurtured and cared for with love, attention, and food: books.

"Priscilla," she heard someone call out.

To her surprise, Stephen was standing beside his buggy under the large oak tree.

"Stephen!" she exclaimed, a smile breaking onto her face. She hadn't been able to spend much time with him since she had begun teaching. While she worked extra hard to help her mamm in the evenings and on Saturdays with chores, Stephen was busy helping his own daed with the barn work and also tending his own farm. This past weekend, she hadn't seen him at all. But he had mailed her a letter, explaining that he was working on some projects that would hinder his weekly visit on Saturday.

"Thought I'd come and visit with the teacher. Mayhaps take her home after school!" he teased.

She flushed, pleased that he was so thoughtful. "That would be right kind, Stephen Esh!"

He helped her into the buggy and, once she was situated, climbed up next to her. His skin was tanned from working outdoors and he looked happy. "How you like the new job, Priscilla?" he asked as the buggy started to roll forward toward the road.

"Oh Stephen," she gushed. "It's ever so wunderbaar! I just can believe how blessed I am!"

He laughed at her enthusiasm. "You are almost a mother to those children, ja? Guiding their learning and their values. I am sure that they all appreciate what they are learning from you. Their parents, too!"

"Even little Katie and Ben have been wunderbaar!" She lowered her voice as she added, "I was worried they might try to take advantage of our relationship."

"Not those two!" he said, chuckling. "Well, come to think of it...maybe a little, they might."

She put her hand on his arm. "Oh but they haven't. Not one bit! Today at lunchtime, I even had a small study session to help two of the Byler children. I was worried that they might harbor some ill will toward me because of..." Her voice trailed off and she averted her eyes. She didn't want to mention Susie Byler's name. That would be gossiping. "But they haven't. They are truly good children, although I'm worried about the younger one, Morgan is his name, who seems to get his letters mixed up. I think he might have a slight learning disability."

At this, Stephen frowned. "You mean like a real disability?"

She nodded. "I don't know much about it but I've heard there are special techniques to help children who mix up their letters. Maybe Daed or the bishop could help me learn more about it."

"I sure hope that, if there is something wrong, you can help correct it," Stephen said. "Have you thought about speaking to Linda Byler? That's his mamm's name, ja?"

Truth be told, Priscilla had thought about going there but wasn't comfortable visiting any Byler farm. She shook her head and averted her eyes. "I'd rather the bishop talk to her. Or, at least, the other teacher."

Stephen frowned. Clearly something was on his mind. "The longer you wait, the longer it will take to get the student help, no?"

There was merit to what he said. "That is true," she admitted.

"But I understand your reluctance to go to the Bylers and discuss such a problem," he said.

She shook her head. "I'm not looking forward to that, ja," she said slowly, trying to pick her words carefully. "But even more importantly, I'm not the regular teacher. If I make such suggestions, they might be misinterpreted. People might think I'm trying to show up the other teacher who may not have noticed."

"Hadn't thought of that," Stephen admitted, frowning as

he stared straight ahead.

For a moment, he seemed deep in thought. He was pondering a solution and Priscilla gave him that time to think. She glanced out of the window at the fields, so perfectly plowed and planted. Green shoots were starting to poke up from the brown furrows of rich soil. If she shut her eyes, she could smell the fresh scent of the earth better.

"I have an idea!" When Stephen spoke, she opened her eyes and returned her attention to him. He was smiling, pleased that he may have found a solution. "Why not write a letter and I can deliver it to the bishop on your behalf? I'm sure to see him before you do, anyway. He can take the letter to the Byler's for you!"

That was the perfect solution! Priscilla clapped her hands together once and smiled, relieved that she could do her duty, both to the struggling student and to her role as a teacher without having to visit the Byler farm. "That's a wunderbaar gut idea, Stephen!" she said. "This way, he can discuss my observations with the regular teacher and they can decide what to do, if anything. I'm just a stand-in teacher, anyway. It should be their decision, ja?"

When they arrived back at Priscilla's home, she hurried inside to draft the letter. Stephen waited outside by the buggy while she sat at the kitchen table, carefully writing her thoughts about the struggling Byler boy and how he kept mixing up his numbers and letters in both math and spelling. She described her own little knowledge about learning disabilities plus what she had read from a book in the schoolhouse. She closed the letter by asking the bishop to determine with the regular teacher whether or not her concerns were valid before speaking with the student's parents.

She reread the letter twice and felt that she had fulfilled her duty as a teacher while protecting herself from anyone thinking that she was prideful. *It's a gut letter*, she told herself as she folded the white piece of paper and slid it into an envelope.

"Here it is," she said as she handed the envelope to Stephen. "I'm ever so grateful for you to take it to him," she said. "I just hope that there is something they can do to help Morgan."

Stephen took the envelope and tapped it against the side of his hand. "Ach vell, at least you tried and that is the first step to solving any problem," he said with a smile. "Now, I must get going. I'll stop by the bishop's farm first but I have my evening chores to do and want to stop at my own farm, too."

She watched as he turned to leave, pausing once as he stopped by the side of the buggy to wave to her.

When he was gone, she stared in the direction that he had disappeared. She was ever so glad that he had suggested writing that letter for the bishop. It would ease her mind to know that someone who was better suited to identify a possible problem with Morgan would be involved. She only prayed that something could be done so that the boy could, one day, read properly.

Chapter Four

It was Sunday before church services when Priscilla heard the first compliments. During the greeting line, when the women entered and shook hands with all of the other women, placing a gentle kiss on their lips, one of the older women smiled and patted Priscilla's arm.

"I heard what a fine job you are doing at the school," Esther said. "Fine job, indeed!"

Priscilla blushed from the praise but didn't have time to say that she was only doing what the regular teacher asked her to do. The compliment had taken her by surprise. She wasn't used to hearing such praise. Yet, since she knew all of the children and their families, it did please her that they seemed to be happy with her efforts to guide their children through their learning while teaching them values and godliness.

When the Millers arrived, Priscilla noticed that Naomi barely spoke to her and gave her a very short, limp handshake before moving down the line and standing next to her cousin, Dorothy, who had already gone through the line. Priscilla frowned, recognizing the cold shoulder from Naomi and the fierce glare from Dorothy.

What did I supposedly do this time, she wondered.

Priscilla remembered only too well how Naomi had pretended to be her friend during the quilting bee two winters ago. Yet, it had been Naomi who had reported information about Priscilla's quilt pattern to Susie Byler. Susie had started a big commotion within the community, claiming Priscilla had stolen *her* pattern. Not once did Naomi apologize for her role in not only aiding the bullying but also for not sticking up for Priscilla.

However, Naomi's mamm took the moment to smile at Priscilla. "Our younger children have the nicest things to say about what a great teacher you are," she said. "Mayhaps you might consider doing it next year, ja?"

"Oh no," Priscilla responded, alarmed at the unnecessary praise. She certainly didn't want people thinking she was proud. "I'm just helping the Teacher until her leg has healed." Besides, she thought, mayhaps I'll be married by then and married women certainly did not teach in the school. There would be too much work to do at their own farm, both inside the house and outside helping Stephen.

During the service, Priscilla sat next to Sarah, Polly, and a young woman named Sylvia. Polly had introduced Sylvia as a cousin from Holmes County, Ohio, who was visiting with her family for a few weeks. Priscilla took one look at Sylvia with her big blue eyes and curly blond hair that poked out from under her prayer kapp and knew that she liked her immediately.

"I heard you are a teacher," Sylvia said to her after the service was over. Her face glowed and her blue eyes sparkled. "That's so impressive! The districts where I'm from only ask the women who have demonstrated the best values and learning. You must be very smart!"

Priscilla shook her hand to ward off more praise. It made her uncomfortable when people said such nice things to her. After all, she was no different than any other woman in the church district. Anyone else would have stepped in to help out the school. "It's not like that," she started. "I'm only standing in while the regular Teacher gets well. She was injured in a horse and buggy accident, you see."

Polly frowned. "Oh Priscilla, you are far too modest! Everyone is talking about some of the new lessons that you have done with the children and how they are all so eager to come to school! I think it's right gut and I'm not afraid to tell you!"

"Polly!" Priscilla whispered, her eyes darting around the room, hoping that no one had overheard.

"Well it's true!" Sarah said, joining the conversation. "And I bet it just burns up that nasty Susie Byler, all this attention you're getting." Sarah leaned over and lowered her voice as she explained to Sylvia, "Susie Byler is fierce jealous of Priscilla and made up all sorts of lies about her, spreading them everywhere. She was even reprimanded by the bishop!"

"Oh my," Sylvia gasped. "I've never heard of such a thing in my own community!" Her eyes looked around the room, trying to find the woman at the center of their conversation. When she spotted the blond young woman, Sylvia narrowed her eyes, squinting in the dim light of the room. "Why would she do something like that?"

"I really don't want to talk about it," Priscilla replied softly. She didn't want to think about the past. It had been a hard summer and an even harder winter. She had thought it was all behind her. Shaking her head, Priscilla sighed and smiled at Sylvia. "There are much more pleasant things to talk about than Susie Byler anyway, ja?"

It was later that evening, however, that Susie Byler's name came up again in conversation. To Priscilla's surprise, it was Stephen Esh who brought up the subject.

He had picked her up from her daed's farm to take her to the youth singing. She could tell right away that he was tense and that something was bothering him. He wasn't looking at her nor was he talking. She could also see that the muscles in his jaw were twitching.

At first, she didn't ask as she felt that it would be prying. But when he missed the turn, she took a deep breath and asked, "What's bothering you, Stephen? I don't mean to intrude but I can see you are right upset about something."

He glanced at her. "I'm sorry, Priscilla," he said. "I really wanted to avoid sharing this with you but I am upset and I just can't hide it."

His tone alarmed her. She had never seen Stephen upset in such a manner. Normally, he was so even-tempered and good-natured. "What is it, Stephen?"

He sighed and shook his head. "I heard something after church service today that really bothered me."

"Oh?"

"Now, I know it's not true but one of the Miller girls was talking with that Susie Byler. They were talking behind me and I think they were talking just loud enough on purpose so that I could overhear them."

At the mention of Susie Byler, Priscilla caught her breath. It had been quiet since the previous winter. Priscilla had thought Susie had learned her lesson after the bishop had reprimanded her and that she wasn't going to bother anyone anymore. Unfortunately, from the look on Stephen's face, Priscilla could tell that this was not going to end well. "What were they saying, if I might ask?"

"Ja vell," he started, stumbling over his words. "Seems

like that Susie is telling people you are a fake and a liar."

That caught Priscilla off-guard and she had to catch her breath. A fake and a liar? Where on earth did Susie keep getting these crazy ideas? She almost wanted to laugh but her heart was racing and she felt angry, instead. "I am having a hard time of believing this!"

Stephen held his hand up, as if the gesture would help calm Priscilla. "I know, I know. Of all people to accuse of such falsehoods!"

"A fake and a liar!" Priscilla didn't know how to respond. How dare that woman accuse Priscilla of the very things that so perfectly described herself? "She's crazy!" Priscilla said sharply. "Plain crazy! What ever is she raving about now? Another quilt pattern?"

Stephen frowned. "It's about the teaching."

Once again, Priscilla was speechless. What did Susie Byler know about her with teaching? The mean-spirited and unchristian behavior of that woman and her insufferable rudeness were truly starting to tax her nerves. "The teaching! Whatever is she possibly accusing me of this time? My teaching doesn't impact her in the least!"

"You won't like this anymore than I do," Stephen said slowly. "It seems that she is telling people that you are not a real teacher. In fact, she said that you marked her cousin's papers low on purpose because you hate her so much. Claims you sent a letter to the bishop asking that her cousin be dismissed from school."

"That's ridiculous!" Priscilla gasped. The accusation was outrageous, indeed. What was most alarming, however, was that Priscilla knew from her past experiences that certain people tended to believe Susie and her horrid lies. "I have done nothing of the sort! In fact, I'm working hard to help Morgan!" *Fake and a liar.* The words rang in her head. Words that were heavy and ugly. "I simply cannot believe it."

"There's more."

"I can hardly imagine what else there could be!"

He cleared his throat as he slowed down the buggy. When it was finally stopped on the side of the road, he turned to face her. "I heard her say that she's going to expose you," Stephen warned. "She was very big on that word. *Expose* you. Repeated it several times." He looked at Priscilla, staring at her with a concerned expression on his face. "You be careful with that girl. We both know what she is capable of doing."

For a moment, Priscilla sat there and seethed. Everything had been going so well in her life, lately. Why did Susie have to start her theatrics and her rantings all over again? Taking a few deep breaths and counting to ten twice, she finally deeply exhaled and looked at Stephen. "I'm just going to ignore her once more. There will come a point in time when she will just tell one too many lies."

"God doesn't like liars," Stephen mumbled, shaking his head in disbelief.

"No one likes liars," she added. She sat back in the seat and stared outside the window.

Stephen clicked his tongue and the horse started to walk down the road again. They rode in silence, each deep in thought. Priscilla tried to clear her mind, not wanting to think about Susie and her lies. Instead, she watched the passing farms.

Each farm seemed so peaceful and quaint. For a

moment, she imagined herself living in one of those farms, surrounded by her own family and experiencing the same peaceful happiness that the people dwelling in them were certainly enjoying. Yet, she no longer held that same peace within herself. Instead, she felt angry and resentful. *That's the Devil talking to you*, she heard a voice say within her head.

"Stephen," she whispered. "I don't feel much like going to the singing tonight."

"I think that's the best place for us to go," he said firmly. "If you don't go, people will think she's telling the truth."

Priscilla knew that he was right. Still, she neither felt like being social nor speculating what other people might be thinking about her. And she certainly didn't want to see Susie! "I'm not thinking nice things about her," she admitted softly. "Perhaps I need to pray a little."

He nodded his head, understanding exactly what she meant. He waited until they passed a large field and brought the buggy to a stop. Quietly, he helped her down and stood back as she climbed up the slight incline, walking away from him. She felt the fading sun at her back. She walked carefully, not wanting to step on any of the newly planted crops. But she also knew that she needed a few moments alone.

Dear Lord, please help me understand how to be a godly woman when my heart feels heavy and angry, she prayed quietly after kneeling down. *Please help me show Susie Byler what it means to be a true Christian by extending a hand of forgiveness to her the way Jesus forgave Judas. Please help me do what I can to help her from whatever is bothering her so much, showing her love in the same way that Jesus forgave the sinners. Guide me so that I can continue to walk in your light and embrace your teachings. Amen.*

Getting up from her knees, she lifted her face toward the sun and, with her eyes shut, she whispered the Lord's Prayer. A bird flew overhead and she felt a cool breeze. She also felt the calming presence of strength and love surrounding her. It was as if a weight had been lifted from her shoulders.

I can do this, she thought.

With a new sense of confidence, Priscilla hurried back to the waiting buggy and smiled at Stephen. "Danke," she said. "I feel ever so much better now."

"Gut." He held her hand as she started to get into the buggy. Yet, he stood in a way so that she couldn't actually squeeze past him. "Priscilla," he said, his voice low and his arm rubbing against hers as he held her hand tightly. "Don't you think it's time we talked to the bishop about baptism?"

"Oh," she whispered, caught off guard for the second time in less than an hour. "Are you saying...?"

"I want us to marry in December, yes."

Priscilla bit her lower lip, staring up into his face. It was the moment she had been waiting for, the moment that she had dreamed about ever since she had known that she loved him. Now, here he stood before her, the early spring crops casting a green glow on the field behind them and the birds chirping as they chased each other through the air. Spring. A season of growth, renewal and change.

"That's only seven months away," she whispered.

"I'd marry you tomorrow if I could," he said, smiling gently at her, his thumb brushing against the back of her hand.

She blushed. What had she done to deserve this wonderful man who cared so much for her? He was strong in faith, even tempered and kind. No one could argue that he was a hard-working man and gave plenty back to the community, sometimes before taking care of himself. Even more important, he was a godly man.

"Stephen," she said, lifting her eyes to meet his. "I will marry you in December."

When he leaned down and gently brushed his lips against hers, she was startled. He had never been so bold before and she wasn't certain how to react. Kissing was best saved for marriage, she had always been told. Still, she couldn't help but think it was a wonderful feeling to have her fiancé, her future husband, kiss her on that beautiful spring evening, just moments after she had promised to be Stephen's Priscilla forever.

"December," he whispered as he pulled back, still staring into her eyes.

"December," she whispered back, her cheeks flushed red and her heart pounding from the joy he had just instilled into her.

When they arrived at the singing, Priscilla felt out of sorts. So much had happened in that short buggy ride. She had learned that Susie Byler was back at bullying again. Yet, Stephen Esh once again had proven that Priscilla had nothing to worry about when it came to Susie. Not only did he not question Priscilla's integrity, he had even asked her to marry him. Such a proposal was not taken lightly among the Amish. Marriage was a forever partnership and with Stephen Esh, Priscilla felt she had committed herself to the best partner in the world.

And then there had been the kiss.

"My word, Priscilla," someone said from behind her.

Looking over her shoulder, Priscilla smiled as she recognized Sylvia, Sarah, and Polly walking toward her. "I hadn't seen you there!" she said.

"You look rather out of sorts," Sarah said, a sympathetic look in her eyes. She lowered her voice and reached out to gently touch Priscilla's arm. "I reckon you heard the latest news about that dreadful Susie Byler," she said, shaking her head.

Priscilla tried to laugh it off. She wasn't going to let Susie's lies bother her, not today and not any day. With a wave of her hand, Priscilla dismissed the gossip. "I don't know what she's trying to get at," she said. "But I'm not wasting one precious moment of life on her silliness. It's her problem and she can deal with it."

Polly raised an eyebrow. "Oh, it's her problem alright. A problem in the head."

The other three women laughed and the subject was quickly changed to something more pleasant and worthy of discussion.

Chapter Five

Back home, Priscilla didn't tell her parents about her decision. After all, it was *her* decision to make and only she could do so. Joining the church was a life commitment. A firm commitment to follow the ways of the Amish and give up any worldliness. For Priscilla, it wasn't something that needed much reflection. She had always shunned worldliness and certainly never considered leaving the Amish community.

But she recognized that her parents were watching her, knowing smiles on their faces. Priscilla suspected that it was because how quiet she was after supper, sitting on the sofa with her crocheting material but getting nothing done as she was thinking long and hard about what it meant to join the church.

Several hundred years earlier, in Europe, their ancestors had given up their lives to follow the Anabaptist beliefs. Others lost their homes and families, all in the name of that commitment to the church. Later, when they began to emigrate from Europe, seeking shelter in the New World, they had struggled to survive. But their faith had helped them. Now, the Amish communities were doubling in size every twenty years. And it was all in the name of renouncing the world in order to honor God.

When she worked in the garden after coming home from the schoolhouse, she often paused, her hands covered in dirt, and stared into the fields. The corn had been planted and was beginning to grow, a gentle blanket of green starting to replace the brown rows of plowed earth. She loved to watch the birds as they hopped between the rows of corn sprouts, dipping their beaks into the ground in hopes of finding a worm or grub.

This life is the way of the Lord, she thought. It pleased her that she would be joining the church and following in the footsteps of her ancestors. There was no other life for her but here, in Ephrata, with her church, her family, and her Stephen. It was plain and it was simple but it was all that she wanted.

It was two weeks later when Priscilla found the courage to approach the bishop after the church service. She had spent these two weeks in reflection and prayer. She had spoken to her parents for guidance and advice. When she knew that she was comfortable with the decision, one that she could not revoke, she had decided to speak with the bishop and request his approval for attending the baptismal instructional that would take place over the summer.

Service had ended and the dinner meal was almost over. The men were beginning to put away the make-shift tables which were really just the service benches cleverly designed into perfectly matching halves that once abutted to each other were transformed into perfectly sturdy trestle tables. The noise of the benches being pulled out of the boards that converted them into these tables, loud as it was, did not cover this of the women conversing jovially while washing the plates and glasses in the kitchen and sorting out the serving sets that some of them had brought along to supplement what was provided by the hosting family for after-service fellowship. Yet, it was a happy noise that spoke of strong fellowship after a morning of faithful worship to God.

"Bishop Zook," Priscilla asked as she approached the older man where he was standing, just outside of the door to the gathering room. "Mayhaps you have a moment?" she asked with her eyes downcast.

He gestured to the men he had been speaking to and they all nodded in the understanding that he needed to speak privately with Priscilla. The bishop and Priscilla took a few steps away from the people gathered outside and preparing to harness their horses to the buggies in order to return home. For most of the families, the afternoon would be spent playing games like Scrabble or Round the World before evening chores. Sunday afternoon was a day for being together and sharing. Later in the evening, the young unmarried people would attend the youth singing. That was a time for some socialization and relaxation among their peers.

But for now, Priscilla was only thinking about talking to the bishop about one thing: her baptismal instruction.

"I'm sorry to interrupt you," she said shyly. "I wanted to speak to you about a matter of great importance to me."

The bishop took a deep breath and pursed his lips, leveling his gaze at her. For a moment, he seemed to be appraising her before he spoke. She wondered what he was thinking as his tired, old eyes surveyed her. Then, with a tilt of his head, he said, "I've heard that things are going right gut at the school. I hope nothing is wrong there."

"Oh no, not at all," Priscilla said quickly, not wanting the bishop to worry that she could be unhappy with the situation at the schoolhouse. Her sincerity reassured him and she was pleased to see him relax.

"That's gut," he said. "I was concerned, Priscilla, for I had heard some whispers about an issue with one of the Byler children. I did receive your letter and spoke with the parents. But now these other stories..." He shook his head, his weathered hand rising to his white beard and tugging gently on it. "Is that what you wish to speak about?"

Again, she was caught off guard. How had he already heard about that? She wondered if Anna, his niece and a friend of hers, had said something to him. She hadn't seen much of Anna recently so she wasn't even certain Anna knew what was being said. "I...I hadn't thought to bring that particular matter to your attention," she stammered. "I certainly know that I didn't write a letter to you asking for the child to be dismissed. In fact, I've been working with him every day, one on one, and seeing some progress...if only in his comfort level."

"That is gut of you," the bishop said, clearly pleased with her efforts.

"Besides, if the parents haven't spoken to me with any concerns regarding how I am helping Morgan, then I take that type of talk as simple gossip," Priscilla added.

To her surprise, the bishop smiled. "As is my feeling, Priscilla. *'Fret not yourself because of evildoers, neither be you envious against the workers of iniquity*[3]*.'* It's right gut advice from the Bible, ja? And something I sense needs to be practiced more by others in our g'may." He stopped walking and turned to face her. "I will be speaking with Susie about her gossip. I will not permit that in this district. Gossip stings of two things that God does not tolerate: lies and pride." His voice was stern and strong.

"Ja," she agreed meekly, feeling awkward as he stood before her. She was surprised by how direct the bishop had spoken to her about the silly rumors that Susie Byler had been spreading throughout the church district and community. She

---

[3] Psalms 37:1

was even more stunned that he admitted that he would be talking with Susie.

"On a different subject, I did some speaking to some people that I know among the Englische," he said. "I told them about your letter and what you noticed about that Morgan boy."

"You did?" That was right gut news indeed. She hadn't heard from the bishop since Stephen had gone to deliver her letter. While she had been working with Morgan Byler as much as she could, she still noticed that he was having difficulties. However, the more kindness and attention that she bestowed on him, the more confident and willing he was to try.

"Seems a lot of good can be done by moving him to the front of the classroom and having him repeat instructions back to you," the bishop said, pausing to tug at his beard. "There is also something called *phonetics* which can help. They are sending me some material which I'd like you to use with the boy."

"Oh that's wunderbaar gut!" She could scarcely contain herself from clapping her hands.

"There were some other tips and advice to help such as visualizing words and using memory tricks," he said. "Now that the issue has been identified, the school board will work with the regular teacher to help him overcome it. Apparently, it's a common learning disability among the Englische. Mayhaps with Amish, too, but we just haven't dealt with it." He smiled at Priscilla, nodding his head as he added, "I'm impressed that you picked up on it. Mayhaps we can help other children, too."

"Danke, Bishop!" she said. She couldn't wait to learn more about how to help little Morgan.

"Now, what did *you* wish to speak to me about then?" he asked in an abrupt manner, changing the subject back on course.

Priscilla's mind seemed to reel. This was the moment. A moment as important as when she had agreed to marry Stephen. It was the moment that would set the rest of her life in motion, When she looked up at the bishop, she took a deep breath and said, "I'm interested in taking the kneeling vow and becoming a baptized member of the church."

Immediately, she felt a weight lift from her shoulders. One Lord, one faith, one baptism[4], she thought. The relief that she felt was almost overwhelming. She was committing herself to God and to the Ordnung, to a life of living "Plain". It was a decision that made her very happy.

The bishop could see the relief in her eyes and reached to pat her hand. "That is right gut, Priscilla. I will be starting the instructionals during service in two weeks. I will be looking for you during the second hymn."

"Danke," she replied. She wondered who else would be joining her at the baptism instructionals. She knew that young women usually attended earlier than young men. She also knew that the youths tended to join just prior to getting married, although some of them took the kneeling vow before announcing their upcoming weddings.

Quite often, when daughters informed their parents that they were going to take the instructional for fall baptism, that was the indication to plant extra large gardens full of tomato plants and celery, two staple ingredients used in the preparation of the wedding feasts. The rest of the congregation

---

[4] Ephesians 4:5

would watch to see which youths left the church worship room for the instructional sessions each Church Sunday during the summer months. The women would whisper their speculations about which of the youths were getting married in November and December.

The only thing that Priscilla hoped and prayed was that one of them would *not* be Susie Byler.

Chapter Six

It was Wednesday evening after supper when the family was relaxing together, sharing the latest news and enjoying each other's company. Priscilla was crocheting some potholders to put into her hope chest while her mamm worked on a baby blanket for a neighbor's new baby girl. Her daed was sitting at the table, enjoying a cup of black coffee while reading the Budget.

She finished her second blue potholder that evening and snipped the end of the yarn with the small scissors that hung around her neck on a twisted thread. Each potholder took her approximately forty minutes to crochet. She was using dark blue yarn for the two that she was working on that evening. Whenever she had more items to add to the hope chest, she still had to go into the attic. But her daed had promised her that he would bring it downstairs. Priscilla couldn't wait. She wanted to see her hope chest every day. It represented her future. Everything that she put into it, from blankets to the wedding quilt to the dainty crocheted table runners were symbolic of the happiness that she hoped to have with Stephen.

"Where did Jonas and David go?" Priscilla asked as she set the potholder on the table, flattening it with her hand.

"Running with their supper gang, no doubt," Mamm said, laughing. "You know those boys. Using the extra daylight to visit with their friends after chores."

In the distance, Priscilla could hear the gentle humming of a horse-drawn buggy approaching from the road. The air was still that evening so noise carried further and clearer. At first, Priscilla ignored it. Buggies often traveled past the farm throughout the day. But when the noise grew louder, Priscilla set down her crochet hook and yarn. She stood up and hurried over to the kitchen window in order to peer outside. From where she stood, she could see the barnyard. There was a buggy in the driveway but the way that it was positioned made it impossible to see who had arrived.

"Got company, Mamm," Priscilla said, looking over her shoulder.

"My word," Mamm replied, setting down her own crochet materials and getting up from her seat. "At this hour of the evening and on a Wednesday?" She clicked her tongue as she joined Priscilla at the window and peered outside. "I hope nothing has happened," she said under her breath. Together, they looked back outside, waiting to see who had come visiting.

"Best go see who it is," her daed sighed, folding the paper neatly before he stood up and walked toward the kitchen door. He reached for his straw hat, sliding it onto his head then opened the door to head outside.

Priscilla and her mamm watched as Daed walked around the side of the buggy. They could see him wave to someone and, after exchanging greetings, he glanced back at the house. Mamm frowned and touched Priscilla's arm. "Something's wrong," she whispered. "Did you see his face?" Without another word, Mamm walked to the kitchen door, waiting to find out what had happened.

Priscilla stayed at the kitchen window. So, when Stephen walked around the side of the buggy, she saw him first. "Mamm, it's Stephen!" she gasped. Stephen had never come calling during the week on an evening. Occasionally, he might stop by on his way home from an errand. But courting days were almost always on the weekends.

The screen door squeaked as it opened. Daed stood there, holding it open, and waited for Stephen to join them. Neither Mamm nor Priscilla said a word. They knew better than to ask. If Daed wanted them to know, he would share the information with them. Instead, they both stood there, waiting for what was surely bad news.

They didn't have to wait long.

Stephen walked into the kitchen first, his face tense and a rolled up paper under his arm. The Budget. He nodded at the women but avoided Priscilla's eyes. That made her feel nervous. What could possibly have happened that would make her Stephen look so stressed?

It was her daed who spoke first. "Priscilla," he said softly, clearing his throat. "We want you to sit down."

Her heart began to race as a dozen different scenarios raced through her mind. Whatever was wrong had to do with her, not the entire family. What could it possibly be? Had something happened to a student? To the schoolhouse? "What is it, Daed?" She looked at Stephen. "Stephen? What's wrong?"

"Seems we have ourselves another little problem with that Byler girl," Stephen said slowly. From the expression on his face, she knew he was struggling to stay composed. "I'm going to show you something but I need you to remain calm, Priscilla."

Calm? "Oh help," she muttered. She shut her eyes and took a deep breath. What had that girl done now? "I don't think I want to know," she said softly. She wished that she could will her heart to stop pounding. Just the mention of Susie's name was enough to send her into a tailspin from heaven toward earth.

"You must hear this," he said, his voice soothing and gentle. "Just know that we will get through this together."

At this, Priscilla opened her eyes and turned to look at him. Whatever it was, she realized, it was bad. She couldn't even begin to imagine what Susie could have done this time. Hadn't she already done enough? And why now? Things had been so good for so long. What could have caused her to start bothering Priscilla again?

Stephen met her gaze this time as he handed her a newspaper to read. Her hands felt something being put into them and, when she looked down, she was surprised to see The Budget. Now, she thought, I'm confused.

"What does The Budget have to do with me or Susie?" she asked, not understanding why he had handed her the paper, the weekly periodical for Amish throughout the country.

Leaning down, Stephen pointed to a section of the folded newspaper. EPHRATA NEWS, it said. Priscilla frowned as her eyes quickly read through the "news" from their town that had been submitted for publication in the Amish newspaper.

"The Byler family reported that the new teacher and her special friend visited their cousin's house to tell them that their son is not able to attend school anymore since he can't learn. The bishop is investigating and is said to be considering shunning the couple from the church district."

Priscilla felt as if someone had physically hit her. The

wind was completely knocked out of her lungs. Her heart raced and pounded inside of her chest. For what seemed like an eternity, Priscilla sat at the table, staring at that paper in her hand as she felt an overwhelming feeling that her heart would leap from her chest. Her eyes re-read the words in complete doubt that she had read them correctly the first time.

When she had a moment to compose herself, she looked up, her eyes wide and full of disbelief. It didn't make sense. She stared at her daed and Stephen, uncertain of what to say. In all of her life, she had never seen anything like this. How on earth could someone just publish something that was complete lies? And in The Budget, of all places!

"Priscilla," Stephen started. However, he, too, was unable to form words.

"I...I don't know what to say," she said, her heart racing inside of her chest. "The bishop is going to shun me?" She stared at her daed and her mamm. Then, the words of the little news article hit her. *And Stephen.* She turned to look at him. "And now she's dragging you into this?" She felt the tears start to swell in her eyes. It was beyond belief that anyone could be so cruel and heartless. "It's all lies!" she whispered.

"We know it is lies," Stephen said. "Everyone will know it is lies. That's all she speaks, Priscilla. Falsehoods and meritless accusations."

Priscilla looked at her parents, her eyes wide and frightened. She needed to know that they believed her. That they, too, knew the words were false. "We never went to her house!" she blurted out.

"Nee," Stephen admitted. "We did not. But I did take your letter to the bishop who must have gone to talk to the parents." He gestured toward the newspaper and scoffed. "This whole thing is complete nonsense."

Her daed clenched his jaw and reached for the paper. While he had been reading The Budget that evening, he hadn't noticed the blurb since it was buried in one of the back pages. "I haven't seen no bishop here," he said angrily, no longer able to control his temper. "If Bishop Zook was going to shun you, he'd be here already! If ever there was an unchristian person in our community, it is that woman!"

Mamm reached for the paper and took a moment to read it. The color drained from her face. "Oh my," she muttered and looked up, staring at her husband. "That woman is plain crazy."

"Something is wrong with her," Daed snapped, throwing the paper back onto the table in disgust. "And I won't stand for it!"

Stephen tried to calm down Priscilla's daed. "Now hold on," Stephen started, his tone respectful despite reproaching Priscilla's daed. "Since this situation has been made public, we need to speak with the bishop about it. Disputes of such a nature are best left to be handled by the authorities of our district and that's Bishop Zook."

"Ja, you are right," her daed said. "Besides, with his name being dragged into it, too, he will certainly have a word or two to say about this matter."

Priscilla stared at the two men, tears starting to stream down her cheeks. She felt shame at the thought that people would read those lies and she knew that they would talk. Some people would even believe it. She had learned that from the issues surrounding her donation of tomatoes for the charity auction and later regarding her quilting bee. "Everyone will read that! They will all know that it is about me! And now she's bringing Stephen into it!"

"I suppose we shouldn't just presume that *she* did it," Stephen said.

"Of course she did it," Priscilla replied, her voice cracking. "Who else would do such a terrible thing?" She wiped at the tears that started to fall from her eyes. "You told me yourself that she had threatened to 'expose' me...whatever that was supposed to mean."

Now that he had calmed down, Daed shook his head. "I'm headed over to the bishop right now," he said, reaching for the paper again. His eyes skimmed the article one last time and the muscles in his jaw tensed. "Someone will answer for this. I've stood quiet for too long in regards to that woman."

"My buggy is hitched already so I can take us there," Stephen said. He looked over at Priscilla and spared her a soft smile to reassure her that all would be well. "Best let us handle this," he said gently. "Don't want you getting involved anymore than necessary, ja?"

She nodded her head, still stunned by the brazenness of that crazy Susie Byler. How dare she publish something so full of lies? What type of Christian person would publish something like this in the media, knowing only too well that it was yet again, one of her ridiculous attempts at making herself look more important and more righteous in the eyes of the readers? What was she trying to prove? That she, Susie Byler, was better than her, Priscilla? That she wanted to be construed as a better person, a better Christian?

Perhaps she believed that denigrating a fellow member

of their community would make her look more important? Or was she just a poor tortured soul that craved all the attention and was feeling jealous because deep down she realized that Priscilla was more successful than her in everything she had considered being her own, guarded "territory" for so long: Growing the best tomatoes, quilting the nicest patterns and, now, providing better guidance to young members of their community than she, Susie Byler, ever could? What was she thinking? Didn't she realize that these unfounded accusations would ultimately cause her own demise? Did she really think that the community was blind, that these readers would not see through her lies and fake accusations?

But Priscilla was strong and pure in her beliefs. As her ancestors had done for nearly half a millennium, she had chosen the Christian way of turning the other cheek and letting God work His remedy as He saw fit. That was the way of the Amish. Yet she could not help thinking that there were other religions with good God-fearing people among them harboring different beliefs than her own. She had read somewhere the expression of "an eye for an eye" and she knew that ultimately Susie's eye would be taken. Her beliefs, however, forbade her to be the one taking that eye and she knew that it would be dealt with through the hand of God. And, reflecting on this, despite the contempt that was threatening to invade her soul, she could not help but feel pity for that self-destructive Susie Byler, this poor tortured soul. It was just a matter of time, she pondered...

When she heard the buggy wheels rattling down the driveway, Priscilla turned to look at her mamm. They were both stunned by what they had seen in the paper, even more stunned that it was anonymous. One could easily submit something to the media under a different name or even ask a friend to do it. . But Priscilla knew better than that. She knew exactly who had submitted that horrid news story, a story full of lies.

The men appeared to be in a rather solemn mood as they walked into the house and hung their straw hats on the pegs by the door. It was Stephen who spoke first as he approached Priscilla who was sitting on the sofa, her hands keeping busy with her crocheting.

He knelt before Priscilla and took one of her hands in his. He brushed his thumb along the back of her hand, staring at it for a long moment as he collected his thoughts. "We went to speak to Bishop Zook. We showed him the newspaper article and what was written. He agreed that it was most likely Susie Byler so he went to her parents' farm," Stephen said. "He wanted to confront her about it."

"Did you go with him, then?" she asked curious about whatever had happened while they were gone.

"Nee," he replied, shaking his head. "Your daed and I waited at the bishop's house. Felt it was better, so that tempers didn't flare."

"What happened, then?" she asked, her eyes wide and sorrowful. Despite the wrong that Susie Byler had done to her, Priscilla still felt some degree of pity for the tormented woman. Her own reflections of the situation made her worry about the woman's mental stability. If there was something wrong with Susie, perhaps she was not entirely to blame, Priscilla had rationalized.

"Susie refused to open the door," he said slowly. He glanced over his shoulder at her daed before he continued.

"Her daed and her mamm were nowhere to be found but the bishop said that he saw Susie looking out the kitchen window when he pulled up and the parents' buggy was parked right out front."

"Oh help!" Priscilla gasped. "She was looking out the window but wouldn't open the door? For the bishop? Didn't she see him?"

Stephen took a deep breath and exhaled. He looked weary from the day's events. It had taken an emotional toll on all of them. "She certainly knew why the bishop was there. Didn't want to face him, I reckon."

Priscilla couldn't imagine what would happen to Susie next. Certainly the bishop would be most irritated at the young woman's behavior. Still, she was not a baptized member of the church. He couldn't reprimand her by putting her on warning or even shunning her. Yet, defying the bishop was a serious matter and one that the bishop would not take lightly, of that Priscilla was sure and certain. "So what did he do?"

"He left a note for the Bylers to visit with him about the matter at hand. That's all he said to us. Not much more he can do until he sees them."

The whole situation seemed surreal. In all of her life, she had never heard of such a thing. How could a person think that she could get away with telling such horrid lies about another? Was her jealousy so strong? Were her insecurities so great? "Well, I will just pray that she gets the help that she needs," Priscilla replied. "I have much better things to do than to worry about that Susie Byler."

With a smile, Stephen covered the top of her hand with his other hand, holding it between his. "The g'may knows the truth. She's pulled her little tricks too often. No one believes her anymore. There is nothing else for you to do but to continue being your sweet, godly self, Priscilla Smucker."

The color flooded to her cheeks. She wasn't used to being complimented. "I'm not any more godly than anyone else," she countered, her eyes downcast.

He stood up, his knees cracking as he did, and turned to her parents. "While I'm here," he said slowly. "I heard a story about a young woman wanting her hope chest brought down from the attic. Mayhaps I could help make that happen, ja?"

It was the perfect thing for Stephen to say to change the mood of the room to a more positive level of energy. Mulling about the reasons behind Susie Byler's actions, as ridiculous as they were, certainly would help no one. Only Susie knew the answers. So, moving on with life was the best medicine for the continued heartache caused by the jealousy of mean-spirited Susie Byler.

Chapter Seven

"She said what?"

It was as if she was replaying a scene from two summers ago.

Priscilla had run into Sylvia and Polly at the Dry Goods Store where she had stopped to pick up some material for a new apron; hers had worn through in too many places to fix. She had also wanted to look for a new hymnbook to teach the children new songs for the end of the year picnic. The parents would be coming and she had an entire program outlined so that the children could entertain their parents before it was time for the dinner meal and a game of stickball in the playground.

Polly shook her head and sighed, her jaw clenched and her expression showing her disgust. "She's telling everyone that it was not the bishop but Stephen that came to her daed's farm and banged on the door, threatening her. She claims that they had to get the bishop involved and that now he really is going to shun you and Stephen."

"Nee, nee," Sylvia said as she shook her head. "That's not what I was told by Naomi and Dorothy. I heard that it was Stephen *and* Priscilla that went to the farm."

"What!" Priscilla felt as if she could scream. "That's ridiculous!" She stared at her two friends, her eyes wide and full of disbelief. The Amish were non-violent by nature. Of course, there were younger men that might be prone to fighting before they took their kneeling vow and older men who were considered a bit strict in their ways. But violence against each other? Unheard of. "Anyone who knows Stephen would realize that it is an outright lie! And I haven't been to that side of town since last March! I have no reason to go there."

"She's telling people that the bishop had to get involved because you threatened her."

At this, Priscilla heard herself laugh. "I did what?"

Several people walking down the aisle smiled at her as they passed. They must have heard her laughing. Many of the Amish girls in the community were serious and quiet so hearing a young woman laugh in public was unusual and drew attention from those people who walked nearby.

"Threatened her," Sylvia repeated.

"Ach vell," Priscilla said. "I'm starting to find her lies humorous. Whoever heard of such a thing? Threatening her?"

"Well, you won't find the next part humorous," Sylvia said. "She's telling people that she's getting a restraining order against you and Stephen."

Priscilla blinked, repeating the words in her head. "A what?"

"A restraining order," Sylvia repeated. "It's an Englische legal document that states you cannot be near her."

She had never heard of that term before and knew that it was not something that had ever been in their Amish community before. Why on earth would Susie do such a thing? "I don't know anything about that," Priscilla said with a frown. "What do you know about it?"

"Well, as I understand it, the police would come to your house and give you a paper," Sylvia explained. "My brother knew about it."

"The police?" Priscilla didn't understand. Could the Englische law do such a thing without speaking to her first? Would they accept Susie's word without question? "Why would she go to the police? I haven't done anything. Besides, Amish don't use the Englische law enforcement!"

"The whole thing is ridiculous," Polly said and, glancing around to make certain no one was nearby, she lowered her voice. "Personally, I think she seems to have an issue wanting attention, even if she had to lie to get it."

Sylvia rolled her eyes. "I have half a mind to say something to her."

Sylvia's words immediately alarmed Priscilla. She knew too well that anyone who came to her defense often felt the brunt of Susie's wrath. Hadn't Anna encountered a bit of the bullying, too, that summer over the charity auction?

"Oh please don't," Priscilla pleaded. "If you do, she might start bullying you."

Dismissing Priscilla's fear with a wave of her hand, Sylvia laughed. "I'd like to see her try!"

With an air of authority, Polly clicked her tongue. "I wouldn't pay any mind to it, Priscilla. Everyone knows by now how deranged she is," she said. "Besides, the only people that pay any attention to her are that Naomi and Dorothy."

Still, the situation didn't sit well with Priscilla. She had never said or acted in any way against Susie. She had never spoken one ill word about her, not even in defense of herself. In fact, she had never had any interaction with this woman before the bullying began over the charity auction.

Speak no ill, even of your enemies, she had always been taught. She also knew that God would protect her, even from

60

slanderous lies from the likes of a misguided young woman in their g'may. Still, as the lies became larger and more ridiculous, it began to wear on her nerves. She simply didn't know how much longer she could stay quiet.

The walk home from the store took her almost thirty minutes as it was two miles from her parents' farm. For the entire walk, Priscilla could think of nothing else besides what she had just been told. She didn't know much about this restraining order claim. Sylvia seemed to think that the police would show up at the farm with this document. The thought of a police car pulling into her parents' lane unnerved her.

Still, knowing that she had done nothing wrong, she had no fear that such a scene would ever unfold. Even the Englische with their worldly ways and nonsensical laws would see through such a falsehood. Not even Susie Byler could spin such a tale full of lies and deceit that the Englische would not be able to see that she was crazy.

When she arrived at home, she noticed that her parents' buggy was gone. They must have gone visiting one of her older sisters. Priscilla set her package on the kitchen table and wandered over toward the side room where Stephen and her daed had put her hope chest earlier the previous week. She ran her hands along the smooth wood and paused, thinking about how this would look at the foot of the bed that she would some day share with Stephen.

She'd have a large garden by the side of the house. Stephen had shown her the exact spot when he had taken her to the farm not so long ago. He insisted that she have the best plot of land so that she could grow her tomato plants. After all, he had teased her, she had grown the most expensive tomatoes in the county.

He had also pointed out the two windows that were in the main bedroom. The bed would go between the windows and the wedding quilt that she had made two winters prior would decorate the bed. It was at the foot of that bed that wore that quilt where the hope chest would be.

She knew that it would be there for their entire marriage. When they had children, she might store keepsakes from their infanthood and school years. She'd keep special letters from family and friends in that hope chest. And one day, God willing, she would prepare both her and Stephen's funeral clothes and leave them in the hope chest for when they passed into God's kingdom.

The hope chest was more than just a place to store things for her new home, she realized. It was a place to store bits and pieces of her life. A happy life began with peace. She knew that from the Bible. She wondered what Susie Byler put in her hope chest, if she even had one. Perhaps that is her problem, Priscilla thought. She just isn't a happy person because she doesn't have peace and without peace, there is no true life.

With a sigh, Priscilla turned around and looked at the empty kitchen. Without her mamm or her bruders in the house, it felt large and lonely. It would feel that way at Stephen's farm, she realized. During the day, Priscilla would be in the kitchen by herself, cooking and canning food with no help from her mamm. In the mornings and evenings, she'd most likely help her husband with the dairy cows, something she had always enjoyed doing with her daed and bruders, too. There would be times during the year when she would help him in the fields, too.

It was almost an hour later when her bruders returned.

She heard the buggy and jumped up from where she had been seated, cutting out the material for her new apron, in order to hurry to the window to see who it was. David unhitched the horse while Jonas walked quickly toward the house. His face was drawn and serious, the muscles in his jaw tensing as he approached.

What's wrong now, she wondered, feeling her heart palpitate as a dozen horrible thoughts raced through her mind.

"Priscilla!" he called out when he flung open the door. "Oh! There you are." He approached her, shaking his head. "I need to tell you something. You should sit first, too."

Priscilla sighed and lifted her hand to stop her bruder. "Is that that nonsense about how I threatened Susie Byler and she has those Englische police coming after me?"

"You heard about that?" Jonas asked, stunned that she was so calm.

"Ja, ja," she nodded her head as she admitted her awareness. "I saw Polly and Sylvia at the store earlier. They told me all about it."

"I heard it from that horrid Naomi Miller and her cousin, Dorothy. They are telling everyone." He leaned against the counter and crossed his arms over his chest. "Did you hear about the not Christian part, then?"

She winced at his words. "The what?"

He raised an eyebrow. "So you don't know it all, then," he said solemnly. "She's telling people that you don't believe in God and that you are worshipping other things...ungodly things."

It took Priscilla a minute to digest what Jonas was telling her. Worshipping other things? That was a lie of all lies and one that would not please God. Not only was she spreading horrible rumors and making waves, she was creating a bad aura around herself. With Priscilla beginning the instructional that very next day, the accusation that she didn't truly believe would reflect more on Susie than on Priscilla.

When will this end, Priscilla wondered. "Is that what she's saying?" she asked, her voice barely a whisper.

"I'm telling you," Jonas said, the tone of his voice sounding angry. "Bishop Zook needs to do something about that woman. She's sick in the head and crazy in the mouth."

There was no denying the truth behind Jonas' words. Yet, something about the way that he said them...the force of emotion behind his claim...that made Priscilla sorrowful. There was something about that Susie Byler that made people behave in a heavy-handed manner. Her antics and behavior seemed to pull people away from God, creating dissention and discord. This type of divide was not healthy and Priscilla wanted no more of it.

Looking up, Priscilla stared at her brother. His face was taunt and his jaw clenched tight. Anger. She recognized the look and knew that she had to stop this before it went any further.

"Pray for her," Priscilla said sharply. "She needs our prayers, Jonas, not our scorn."

He glared at his sister. "How can you be so kind hearted as to even care about that horrid woman?"

Defiantly, Priscilla lifted her chin and stared at her bruder. How could he ask such a question? Did not Jesus forgive his persecutors, even as he hung on the cross, his earthly life ebbing from his body as he prepared to join his father? "Because God wants us to forgive her and pray for her."

As her words hit him, his shoulders slumped and he lowered his eyes. Priscilla felt bad for snapping at her brother as she reminded him of what was truly important. It wasn't that Susie Byler continued to slander her good name and reputation. No, Priscilla thought. It is a test from God to see how we respond to such a person. Do we talk with our mouth but not act with our hearts, she asked herself.

"You are right," Jonas said. "Her sins need to be forgiven by everyone, not just you."

"I suggest that we pray together," Priscilla said and reached for her brother's hand. He hesitated before he took her hand, reluctantly acquiescing to her suggestion.

Silently, they bowed their heads and prayed.

Chapter Eight

It was the next day before church service when Priscilla had a moment to speak with her friends. Susie was standing on one side of the kitchen, surrounded by Naomi and Dorothy, their faces locked in a grimace as they periodically glanced over their shoulders at Priscilla.

Priscilla ignored them and hurried over to join Polly, Sarah, and Sylvia. They wanted to talk about Susie Byler but Priscilla shook her head, not wanting to waste one more minute of her precious happiness thinking about Susie.

Her heart had shifted the day before when she had prayed for Susie with her brother. It was as if the burden of the problem left her shoulders and moved elsewhere. Priscilla suspected it moved onto Susie's, especially if the angry scowl on her face was any indication.

Priscilla noticed that Susie's mamm had not attended the service that day. In fact, as she thought about it, she realized that Susie's mamm hadn't been to church for over a month. She wondered if her mamm was ill, perhaps from knowing what her dochder was doing and what the community was saying about her.

"Oh," she said out loud. "I forgot something in the buggy!" She smiled at her friends. "If you'll excuse me. I dare not forget it and will need it for the service."

Polly raised an eyebrow and, with a knowing smile, nodded her head: *En Miener Jugen*, the devotional book for youths seeking to take the baptism. Sarah and Sylvia didn't catch up and for that, Priscilla was grateful.

She hurried outside, past the clusters of men that were talking before the service. This was the time when everyone got together and shared stories and news. The women tended to congregate in the kitchen of the house where the service was being held while the men stayed outside or in the barn, depending on the weather.

The buggies were parked all over the yard and driveway. She had to peek at the backs of them to try to identify her daed's. Jonas and David had arrived later, having ridden in David's buggy. She suspected they were going to visit their friends after the fellowship meal.

"Priscilla!" someone called out.

She spun around, startled by the interruption. But, when she saw it was Stephen, she smiled and immediately approached him. "Gut mariye!" she called out, waving.

He waved back but did not speak. His face looked serious and she wondered if something was wrong. When they stood before each other, he averted his eyes and shuffled his feet, apparently nervous about whatever he wanted to say. She had never seen him look like this and it worried her.

"Are you not well?" she asked, her own anxiety starting to rise in her throat.

"Nee, that's not it," he said, his voice catching on itself. "I have something for you." He glanced around to make certain no one was watching and he reached into his jacket pocket for a folded piece of white paper. "I want you to read this when you can during the service...not before, ja?" he said, thrusting the paper into her hand before, his eyes still not meeting hers, he hurried back to rejoin the men.

She stared at the piece of paper, her heart pounding

inside of her chest. Was it a bad news letter? Was he canceling their upcoming marriage? Had the stress of Susie Byler and her lies gotten to Stephen? She lifted her eyes and sought out Stephen in the crowd of men but she couldn't see him. His back must have been to her and, despite his height, she couldn't find where he stood.

Clutching the letter, she made her way to the buggy to find her devotional. With a heavy heart, she walked back to the farmhouse where the church service was going to be held. He had told her to read it during the service. She knew that she couldn't read it first. He had been very specific about that. The next fifteen minutes would feel like an hour as she worried that her future was about to be turned upside down.

"What happened?" Polly asked when Priscilla finally returned. "You are drained white as a sheet!"

"You ill?" Sarah asked, concern on her face for her friend.

"Nee, nee," she said, shaking her head. She couldn't possibly tell her friends about the letter and how she suspected that Stephen Esh was breaking off their engagement. Frankly, Priscilla didn't know which would be worse: the humiliation or the heartache of losing Stephen Esh after all that they had been through.

The room grew silent as the bishop and deacons entered the room, followed by the host and his older brother and aging father. Hosting church Sunday was often a big day for the family and their parents and siblings often came to help them set up prior to the event and they almost always attended the service.

The men walked along the line of women and shook

each woman's hand in greeting. They looked stern and serious, no smiles or warmth in the ritual reception. Once the bishop and deacons finished greeting the women, they walked into the room where the benches were lined up and took their seats in the middle, facing each other.

The older and married women walked into the room next, the elderly leading the line with the oldest women at the head. It was a honor to be the oldest woman, a position of great respect among the community.

Next, the older and married men entered the room and sat down on the opposite side of the room from the woman. They sat facing each other, not the front of the building. They would sit for almost three hours on hard, wooden benches in a room that had no fans or air conditioning. By the end of the service, the room would be stifling hot and most of the worshippers would have fought off sleep at least once or twice during the past hour.

When the single people had filed into the room and taken their places at the back of the respective sides, which were separated by gender, the bishop gave a signal and all of the men took of their hats, placing them under the bench where they were seated. It was a fluid movement as they all did it at the same time and the official indication that service was now beginning.

The opening hymn was started by a man seated in the back. He began the hymn by singing the first syllable to a special tune. The rest of the congregation would join in to complete the entire line. Then, the man would begin the next sentence in the hymn. Priscilla loved listening to the voices of the church meld together, lifted up in praise of their God and savior Jesus Christ. While she enjoyed the sermons, too, she found herself anticipating the singing the most.

> All you Christians, you who are pure,
> Rejoice from your hearts,
> Through Jesus Christ, that God is
> Granting us faith, love, and hope.
> Because of this we constantly
> Hope without ceasing,
> That what God promises through His Spirit
> Shall soon be revealed to us.
>
> The promise in Jesus Christ is
> To live with Him eternally.
> Yes, all those who here believe,
> And do not resist His Word,
> For them He has prepared a city.
> Those who are received by the Father,
> For them there is joy forever.
> Its light shines as the sun[5].

It was the perfect hymn to start the service. After all, today was the day when she would give herself to Christ by starting her baptism instructionals. The words touched her heart and she looked around the room at the serene faces that stared at the bishop as they lifted their voices together, unified in verse and faith.

She smiled as she watched some of the smaller children begin to fidget. Seated ahead of her, Martha Yoder had her smallest child on her lap, the little girl's head pressed against her shoulder. Her two older daughters sat on either side of her

---

[5] Ausbund, Song 106 verse 1-2

while her son, Melvin, sat across the room next to his father, Menno. It always amazed Priscilla how the children always behaved during church service. Rarely were their outbursts and those were limited to the infants and youngest toddlers.

The song ended and the bishop signaled that it was time for the instructional class to leave the room while one of the deacons gave a sermon. This was the moment when those members of the community made public their commitment to join the church to the entire congregation. Parents would learn for the first time about their child's decision to take the kneeling vow and officially become Amish. It was a beautiful moment for those parents who, with joy in their hearts, watched as their children made the public decision to begin the journey toward baptism.

Priscilla clutched her devotional in her hand and felt the edge of the white paper that Stephen had given to her. She had forgotten about the letter and she wondered if she would have a moment to read it while in the other room.

Best not, she told herself. She didn't want to fight tears while in the other room with the bishop.

Several other young men and women stood up and began to walk out of the worship room, following the bishop into a private room where he would talk to them about the importance of baptism and what it meant to commit to a Plain life. Priscilla smiled as she recognized one of the young men as her brother's friend, Jacob. She hadn't looked around at the women, feeling too conspicuous of the eyes that were watching her leave the room.

And then she saw her.

Susie Byler had stood up and was walking to join the

small group. Priscilla glanced around the room and noticed that her daed and brothers were watching the procession. They, too, had noticed Susie Byler and realized that Susie Byler had requested to attend the baptismal instructions, too.

Priscilla felt the color drain from her face. How could she face the next twelve weeks of instruction, seated in the same room as Susie? How could she kneel next to her on that very special day and take her vow to join the church with Susie Byler at her side? For a second, she panicked but, in that moment, her eyes caught sight of Stephen. He was staring directly at her, a serene look on his face. His eyes shone and he smiled at her, the solemn expression on his face from before completely transformed into one of peace and tranquility.

She glanced at the letter in her hand. What had he written to her? Why had he been so nervous? Perhaps she had misunderstood his intention. She vowed to read that letter as soon as she had a moment's peace to see what it was that Stephen wanted her to know.

"Not you," the bishop said.

Priscilla looked up, startled by the words that came from the bishop's mouth. He was blocking the doorway into the other room and she couldn't walk past him. "Me?" she asked, her voice almost squeaking in disbelief. Was the bishop not permitting her to take her baptismal instruction after all? She felt a wave of heat cross her cheeks at the shame of such a thought.

"Nee," he said and glanced over her shoulder. Priscilla was confused and turned to look in the direction of his gaze. To her surprise, Susie Byler was standing right behind her. Priscilla felt her heart lurch in her chest when she realized that the bishop was speaking directly to Susie.

"What do you mean?" Susie asked, her eyes flashing angrily, first at the bishop then at Priscilla.

"Nee, Susie Byler," the bishop repeated. "You will not be taking your instruction this year."

Several people in the congregation had overhead this statement and there was some whispering among the women. Priscilla glanced over at her family, first at her mamm then to the other side of the room at her daed, brothers, and Stephen. They were watching the scene unfold with intense curiosity.

"Why ever not?" she demanded.

"You know exactly why not!" The bishop's voice boomed loud enough for everyone in the room to hear. Priscilla shrank against the wall, not liking being in the middle of this conversation. "Your lies have caught up with you for what needs to be the last time. Until you repent and apologize to everyone for what you have done, you will be denied your baptism. Only the pure of heart can receive the Lord and I have heard how impure your heart truly is!"

"It's her," Susie hissed under her breath. "She has that lying serpent tongue!"

"Enough," the bishop warned. "You've slandered her for the last time with your false claims of threats and lies about legal restraints."

"They aren't lies!" she demanded but the color was flooding to her cheeks.

"Then where are they?" He raised an eyebrow. "You've been claiming this restraint for weeks now. Oh ja, I have been aware of it. But I also know how the Englische system works. There has been no restraining order against Priscilla! Perhaps you made one up, signed a piece of paper or something, but it has never been confirmed or delivered by the Englische authorities...nor will it."

"They couldn't find her," Susie said meekly, trying to salvage some shred of dignity. "It will come."

"Nee," the bishop said. "It will not come."

Susie lifted her chin defiantly, staring at the bishop.

"Furthermore, if you had gone to the authorities," he continued. "The Englische authorities, it just shows that you are not prepared to follow the Ordnung and shun worldliness. Had these things truly happened, you would have handled them as a Christian, a true Christian. Instead, you have hidden behind lie after lie for years."

"She is not the true Christian," Susie said, her voice sharp and angry. "Why is no one doing something about her?"

"Perhaps it is because you have shown everyone in this congregation that what you claim against Priscilla is actually a projection of yourself. Of your own shortcomings!" He looked around the room at the other members. "A house divided cannot stand," he said. "And I will no longer have strife and division in our district. While Susie Byler has not taken her baptism yet and, therefore, cannot be shunned, she will, however, be denied the kneeling vow and asked to not attend our worship services. The bishop of the next district has agreed that the Byler family may attend there." He leveled his gaze at Susie, enunciating his last words with strength and conviction "But no longer here."

There was a collective gasp in the room and the murmuring continued in the background, followed by a heavy silence. Priscilla felt her heart start to race as she heard all of this. Once again, the bishop was protecting her against Susie's vicious attacks. She was grateful for his support but she felt pity for the shell of the woman that had just been all but shunned, banished from her community and church district.

Out of respect, Priscilla lowered her eyes. She couldn't look at Susie Byler, knowing that the girl had been publicly shamed for her deeds.

Her eyes fell on the white paper that was poking out from the devotional. She unfolded it and skimmed over the lines written in a very neat ink:

My dearest Priscilla,

Today is the beginning of the rest of your life, a life that will be bound to God and our Christ. It is an honor to know that in less than six months, you will be my wife. I will watch you today with both pride and love as you begin this journey to commit yourself to the church as I know that your next commitment will be to me. I am humbled by your choices.

Your loving brother in Christ,

Stephen

Her eyes shot up and she scanned the congregation until she saw Stephen. She wished that she could talk to him, to apologize for having doubted him. She felt ashamed that she had thought he was ending their relationship. Tears came to her eyes and she had to blink them away. She held the letter against her chest and knew that it was something she would treasure forever. She tucked it into the devotional as she followed the bishop into the room, leaving Susie Byler standing outside the door, her mouth hanging open and the rest of the congregation staring at her.

It was after the worship service when Priscilla found a moment to bend her head next to Sarah. "What happened?" she whispered, not wanting anyone to know that she was talking about what had happened earlier. However, she also knew that most everyone was whispering about how Susie had been banished from the church district.

"She wouldn't leave at first but the congregation just sat there, averting their eyes," Sarah said. "Her daed finally got up to leave, yanking her by the arm. If it was anyone else but Susie, I would have felt bad for her."

"I've never heard of a bishop doing such a thing," Priscilla whispered back. "Have you?"

"Nee! But at least now you don't have to worry about Susie Byler!"

"One would hope," Priscilla responded, not exactly agreeing that anything would stop Susie.

Polly joined them as they stood by the table with the pitchers of water. While the first seating ate, the younger women would refill bowls with food and glasses with water. For the moment, no one needed anything.

"You won't believe what that Naomi Miller just said to me," Polly said in a hushed voice. "She told me that she had never believed Susie and not once said an unkind word about Priscilla!"

"Oh help!" Priscilla mumbled.

"She said that, then?" Sarah asked in complete disbelief that Naomi would deny having been involved. "Why, I've heard her myself! Her and that horrid cousin of hers, Dorothy, have supported Susie Byler from day one!"

"Her version of the truth seems to change from one day

76

to the next, ain't so?" Polly added, clicking her tongue and shaking her head. "Funny thing is that she can't even be shunned properly, not as a true Amish woman."

For the rest of the fellowship hour, the girls tried to avoid the topic of Susie Byler. There was a general tension in the air because of what had just happened. No one was certain how to react. However, most people knew the underlying reasons for the bishop's decision. The history of how Susie had continually attacked Priscilla was certainly not unknown.

After the members of the church had finished their dinner meal, the women scurried to clean up the dishes while the men disassembled the tables, converting them back into the wooden church benches and folding the legs underneath. Now that they were flattened, the benches could be stacked neatly into the plain, grey wagon outside where they would be stored until the next church service.

The children were outside playing, chasing each other throughout the front yard. Slowly, people began to say their good-byes and gather up their young ones to return to their own farms. There would be an afternoon of games or visiting with others before the evening chores would need to be completed. As to Priscilla, she knew that Stephen would pick her up later and take her to the singing , which many among the other young adults from their district would attend.

"You read my letter, then, ja?" a voice whispered in her ear.

Startled, Priscilla spun around and accidentally bumped into Stephen who was standing behind her. He reached out to grab her arm so that she wouldn't stumble backwards. "Oh Stephen!" she gasped. "You gave me quite the fright!"

A smile crossed his lips. "You read it, ja?"

She blushed. "Ja," she admitted, her hand clasping the book in her hand where the letter was safely stored. "I will treasure your words forever. I will put this letter in my hope chest with all of my other important memories."

That pleased him. She could tell by the way he looked at her. "I am so humbled, Priscilla," he started. "We have such an amazing future together and it officially began today. You have started your journey to yield to your higher authority."

She hadn't thought of it that way. "*Gelassenheit*," she whispered, referencing the cornerstone of the Amish way of life: the yielding to God in complete self-surrender, with contentment and a quiet spirit.

He nodded in agreement. "Ja, *Gelassenheit*."

Chapter Nine

The sun was shining in the sky for the end-of-year picnic at the little schoolhouse. Priscilla had made certain that the one large classroom had shone, sparkling clean. She had spent all day on Saturday scrubbing the floor, walls, and windows. Stephen had even come to help her, making sure that the furniture was moved so that every inch of the floor shone as bright as the sun.

When the parents had arrived, they sat at their children's desk, anxiously awaiting the end of year concert of hymns and poems that Priscilla had taught their children. On each desk was a folder of the children's work that had been done during the year. Priscilla had managed to find samples of the students' work from early in the year and added these in the folders.

Stephen and her parents had come, too, eager to see young Katie and Ben but also to support Priscilla on her final day as the substitute teacher for the school.

The pageant had gone flawlessly, despite Ben forgetting a line of his poem. All of the parents had applauded each child's efforts and, when the event was over, the students had shyly presented Priscilla with a handmade book, each page consisting of a personal letter from each student, thanking her for being such a great teacher to them. The gift had touched her in a way that she couldn't explain. Each one of the students held a very special place in her heart. She would never forget her short stint as a teacher and was ever so glad Bishop Zook had asked her to take over the position.

"Priscilla," someone said as the children and parents

were headed outside for dinner under the trees and a game of stickball.

She was surprised to see Linda, Morgan Byler's mamm approach her. At first, Priscilla glanced around for Stephen or her daed, worried that Linda was going to confront her about the Susie Byler situation. But the smile on Linda's face spoke otherwise of her intentions.

"I want to thank you for helping my Morgan," Linda said. She reached out and grabbed Priscilla's hand. "Your work with him for his reading is ever so appreciated! And his progress...I see remarkable changes in him."

"I'm so glad to know that," Priscilla said, stilling her beating heart. "There are great tricks to dealing with dyslexia," she admitted. "I found a lot of resources that I will leave for the regular teacher."

Linda nodded. "Danke for sharing," she said. "And danke for caring. You know my niece has that dyslexia, too. Can't see the words right." She shook her head and lowered her voice, a clear indication that whatever was about to be said was not meant for others to hear. "Such a shame, too, since her mamm wasn't always right nice about Susie not being able to read and getting her words all mixed up. Thought she was right dumb." Linda shook her head and added, "Wish her teacher could have been as wunderbaar gut as you are."

Linda's comment stunned Priscilla. Since Susie hadn't lived in their community growing up, Priscilla hadn't known her. Indeed, it was after Susie's grandparents died in Florida that Jacob had moved his wife and daughter back to Pennsylvania and taken up farming in the same district as one of his brothers. So Priscilla knew very little about Susie and her childhood. She also knew very little about Susie's parents.

"I didn't know that," Priscilla managed to say. So Susie hadn't been diagnosed as having dyslexia as a child? She most certainly had struggled in school and probably did poorly. That, for sure and certain, would have hurt her self-esteem, Priscilla realized, especially if her mamm teased her or said mean things about Susie not being able to read properly. If Susie had grown up thinking that she was stupid, it would certainly have negatively impacted her psyche, she realized.

"Ja," Linda said. "It's true."

"Well," Priscilla struggled to find words to convey what she was feeling . Part of her felt sorry for Susie Byler. She had suffered during her childhood, that was apparent. However, the other part of Priscilla knew that choices were made by a grown woman who knew right from wrong. "I sure hope that Morgan is able to receive help" she heard herself say.

Linda started to walk away but turned back, dipping her head as she lowered her voice again. "And I sure do apologize for all of those things that she has done to you. Ain't quite right, that girl. Maybe now she can get some proper help, ja?" Linda didn't wait for a response as she hurried to rejoin her family.

Priscilla stared after her, realizing that more people knew about the problems and the source behind those problems than she had realized. Despite the pretense of godliness, Susie Byler was anything but that...and people knew it. That realization seemed to give Priscilla a new sense of peace. She felt as if she understood, now, that lies and falsehoods could never win. She hadn't given the community enough credit, that was for sure and certain.

"What a wonderful program, Priscilla!"

She turned around and smiled as Stephen approached her. He was carrying two plastic cups filled with meadow tea. "I was nervous," she admitted. "Do you think it went well, then?"

He handed her one of the cups. "Oh ja, for sure! And I was impressed by Morgan being able to read that verse. You've truly done a wunderbaar thing, helping that boy."

Demurely, she lowered her eyes. "It's his efforts that did it, not mine."

"It was your encouragement," he countered.

"It's what I was hired to do," she stated, ending the flow of compliments. "I was quite pleased with the children today. They really adapted well to the disruption and their respect in the classroom was a right gut testimony to their regular teacher."

Several other parents came up to Priscilla, shaking her hand and thanking her for a job well done with the children and their learning. Everyone seemed to be beaming at her, reminding her that she had touched the lives of more than the children...she had touched the lives of the families in the district as well.

In many ways, she realized that each of the children was like her precious hope chest at home. In the beginning, they were empty vessels, waiting to be filled with goodness and godliness. The values that the children learned from school, church, and family helped them become positive influences on the entire district. The past few weeks of teaching the children had helped to contribute something to their lives, something that they would put into their own "hope" chest, something to reflect upon over the years.

When the children had all left with their parents,

Priscilla walked into the schoolhouse for one last time. She knew that she would not be returning until her own children attended the school. Her short time as a teacher had been a blessing to her, something wonderful to tuck into her heart, the same way that she would put the compilation of letters from the students into the bottom of her hope chest. They would reside there, safe amongst her other keepsakes, and, one day, would be shared with her own children and eventually their children.

She wiped clean the board one last time, using water from the pump in a bucket that Stephen had bought inside for her. She made certain to wash each of the desktops and organize the books. It didn't take long, especially since she had cleaned over the previous weekend.

Collecting her things, she walked down the aisle between the desks and headed toward the door. She paused one last time as she looked back, her mind filled with the memory of the children sitting there, reading from their books or raising their hands to answer a question. She would miss it and almost wished that she had more time to teach. However, she knew that she would be busy over the next few months, helping her daed and mamm around the farm. She needed to focus on the garden and canning food for the winter. They would can even more food than usual since some of those goods would be used at her wedding feast.

"Ride for the teacher?"

She laughed as she heard Stephen call out to her. He had parked his buggy under the tree and was leaning against the side, his straw hat tipped back on his head. She locked the door to the schoolhouse and walked down the steps toward him.

"Were you waiting the whole time, then?" she asked, her voice happy and light.

"Ja," he said, reaching out to take the bundle of books that she held in her arms.

"You shouldn't have done that," she said. "I know you have so much work to do at your farm."

He smiled and gently corrected her. "Our farm."

She blushed and averted her eyes, hoping that he didn't see the glimmer of pride that flashed there. She would never be able to fully suppress her happiness with Stephen Esh. He was a right gut man and God had smiled on her when He guided Stephen in her direction. "Not yet," she whispered.

After he slid open the door to the buggy, he set the books on the back seat and turned to help her crawl inside. Once situated, she smiled at him as he sat next to her. "Now," he said, releasing the brake to the buggy and lifting the reins. "How about a treat for Teacher? Perhaps some nice ice cream for a warm spring day?"

"Why, that would be wunderbaar!" she said, bouncing slightly on the blue velour seat of the buggy as he backed up the horse. "And then we can read these letters from my students before I tuck them into my hope chest," she added with a warm smiling, hugging the package of letters.

The sun was still overhead as the buggy pulled away from the schoolhouse. She glanced back, sad that her time as a schoolteacher was over. It had been such an enjoyable experience.

But a moment later, the strange feeling gave place to one of relief and fulfillment.

It finally dawned on Priscilla that by not directly

confronting Susie Byler when she had spread her lies within the community, Susie had not achieved her goal of discrediting her. Indeed, Susie had actually made Priscilla a stronger and a better person, a person of such high moral fiber that she had been honored with the privilege to being asked to teach those children.

By turning the other cheek and trusting that God would work His wonderful ways, she had embraced the very essence of her faith and proven not only to others, but to herself as well that she was pure of heart and rightful in deeds. She had grown even closer to God, closer to her community and closer to this wonderful man who had stood by her all along, the man who would soon become her beloved husband and the devoted father of their children.

Priscilla turned to look out the window, happy as she realized that she had come a long way during the past two years and grown. In many ways, the experiences with Susie Byler had taught her to survive by trusting in and walking with God in ways that she hadn't known were possible.

As happy as she was with the prospect of a strong, fulfilling future with Stephen, she was most happy that she had developed such a strong relationship with God. While she tucked her precious earthly treasures into her beautiful hope chest, she was most pleased that she could carry that precious relationship with God within her heart.

Book Discussion Questions
By Pamela Jarrell, Administrator of The Whoopie Pie Book Club on Facebook

Question #1: Why do you think the Hope Chest was so important to Priscilla?

Question #2: The bishop approaches Priscilla's daed about teaching the local school while the regular teacher recovers. Why is that position so important to the Amish community?

Question #3: Priscilla notices that one of the students has a learning disability. How do you think the Amish recognize and deal with such situations, given that their teachers receive no special training nor do they have access to special resources?

Question #4: What triggered Susie to begin to bully Priscilla again after such a long period of time of have left her alone? Why do you think she included Stephen and the bishop in her web of lies?

Question #5: Unlike the previous books, where Susie spreads gossip among the community, she decides to elevate her bullying to a new level by posting that "news" in the Budget, the Amish newspaper. What was she trying to achieve by doing so?

Question #6: What do you think Polly meant when she said that Susie could not even be shunned properly?

Question #7: In the end, Priscilla realizes that she has grown stronger in her relationship with God. Is there a particular moment (or moments) in the story where you can identify contributors to this relationship?

Love reading Amish romances and Amish Christian fiction?

Please join the Whoopie Pie Book Club Group on Facebook where members share stories, photos, book reviews, and have weekly book club discussions.

One More Thing...

I want to personally thank you for reading The Hope Chest. I hope you enjoyed reading it as much as I enjoyed writing it. Please note that the next novella in the series, The Clothes Line, is scheduled for release in Summer 2013.

If you enjoyed this book, I'd be very grateful if you'd post a short review on Amazon. Your support really does make a difference to me. Not only do I read all the reviews in order to see what you liked and how I can improve, it also motivates me. When I hear from my readers and fans, it really makes me want to keep writing...just for you.

If you'd like to leave a review for The Hope Chest on Amazon, simply click here. Additionally, if you'd like to see a list of my other books on Amazon, click here (http://url.ie/guop).

With blessings,

Sarah Price

http://www.facebook.com/fansofsarahprice

ABOUT THE AUTHOR

The Preiss family emigrated from Europe in 1705, settling in Pennsylvania as the area's first wave of Mennonite families. Sarah Price has always respected and honored her ancestors through exploration and research about her family's history and their religion. At nineteen, she befriended an Amish family and lived on their farm throughout the years. Twenty-five years later, Sarah Price splits her time between her home outside of New York City and an Amish farm in Lancaster County, PA where she retreats to reflect, write, and reconnect with her Amish friends and Mennonite family.

Find Sarah Price on Facebook and Goodreads!
Learn about upcoming books, sequels, series, and contests!

Contact the author at sarahprice.author@gmail.com.
Visit her weblog at http://sarahpriceauthor.wordpress.com or
on Facebook at www.facebook.com/fansofsarahprice.

CPSIA information can be obtained
at www.ICGtesting.com
Printed in the USA
LVHW082038220221
679649LV00049B/3250